What Is Given

Brit Washburn

Wet Cement Press

Asheville & Berkeley

What Is Given ©2025
by Brit Washburn
ISBN 979-8-9883840-9-0

Library of Congress Control Number:
2025932575

This view of the wet woods edition

Acknowledgments:

Thank you to the editors of the following
publications in which some of these poems
first appeared: *The Asheville Review, Main-
tenance of Way, Mountain Xpress, New York
Quarterly* & *Wet Cement Magazine*.

Thanks, also, to Alex, Barbara, Ed, Holly,
Lisa, both Maras, Mildred, Miriam, Nick,
Rick, Sebastian, and Thoreau, for all they
have given.

Wet Cement Press
1908 Yolo Ave
Berkeley, CA 94707

CONTENTS

Dear love, I would have said
(And to each bird who flew up from the wood),
I would be gentler still if that I could,
For on this Easter morning it would seem
The softest footfall danger is, extreme. . .
And so I prayed to be less than the grass
And yet to feel the Presence that might pass.
I made a prayer. I heard the answer, "Wait,
when all is so in peril, so delicate!"

—May Sarton

IN THE CLEARING

I meant to make note
of how, during a snow-
storm a couple of weeks
ago, the south and west
sides of the lake were sheltered
by a stand of trees, the north
and east exposed so that,
when I came around the bend,
sleet and hail stung my face,
and it became an effort
to lean into the wind.

But then, out again
the next day, those same
places that had been
undercover, in shadow, were now
frozen solid, a obdurate crust and black
ice making the path treacherous,
while in the clearing, where
the elements had been
worst, sun had begun
to thaw the hard earth,
slush and mud an easier
surface to navigate,
a softer, safer place
to find my footing. I was sure
this meant something.

Part I

What Is Given

Making Doughnuts During Quarantine

First, measure raw sugar into a blender,
add dried lavender and lemon zest, pulse
until a fragrant dust
begins to rise from the machinery.

Set this aside
for at least four hours
or, better yet, a month. It's okay
if you haven't planned accordingly.
It's ok if you haven't planned.

Use this time to make
a cup of tea, let it steep,
breathe, proceed.

Once you can wait no longer, stir
vinegar into almond milk,
allow it to curdle, add
melted coconut oil, vanilla,
sifted flour, salt, leavening,
every regret that can't be buried
out back, burned in a bonfire, sent
down river without a raft.

While they bake, the scent
will waft through the house

like linens laundered and line-dried,
tied together to make the rope
you've shimmied down, a note
left by the cooling rack, saying
"take and eat, this is my body
given for you, do this
in remembrance of me."

WHAT IS DIVINE

Not this confection,
despite its sweetness
and what its name may claim,
not really.

Nothing that can be taught
in school, no institute
of higher learning.

Intervention, ordinance, right?
All things inexplicable, indefensible,
frightening.

The light on the kitchen table,
the way it plays off the crystal
sugar bowl, the glass salt cellar,
clears the air even before
our quarrel is over.

Forgiveness, perhaps, though
that can be as unfathomable
as the rod detecting water underground—
unseen, silent, but exerting
a pull that tilts the branch
toward the source, somehow,
if you believe such things.

And patience—the capacity to accept,
without upset, delay, trouble, suffering.
The mercy chaplet, prayed
at the hour of death.

Patience, my child, patience.

Memento, Spring 2020

On the table, a platter
of late-season citrus, slightly rank;
a carafe of wilting snowdrops, plucked
from the yard, their heads bowed in
    acquiescence.

A screwdriver, for some reason;
a book, and, in the background,
the sound of the dishwasher running,
a girl of ten talking on the phone with a
    friend.

Early evening, early April,
a chill in the air but sunny
outside where you and the boys
reinforce the fence
around the goats' grazing grounds
down the slope behind the house.

I am about to roast cauliflower,
toast walnuts, chop parsley,
toss these with pasta. Then
we'll sit together and talk
of today's news of the plague:
my father's acquaintance
who succumbed, the number of confirmed
cases in the county, whether it is worth

the risk to run out for provisions,
if they can even be had, how long
our supplies will last, and when
the lockdown might end.

Afterward, we'll deliberate
over what to watch until
we're nearly too weary
to watch anything at all. Still,
we'll settle side by side on the sofa
for the sake of shaping the day,
the solace of staring straight ahead,
nothing to face but what's in front of us.

PICTURE

Laundry wrinkling in the dryer.
Dishes in the sink, a spent tea bag
staining the enamel. The garbage,
compost, recycling—all of these

will be there, where you leave them,
long after the sky has darkened and
the rain has come, long after
the sun has set.

Forget, if you can,
a sense of urgency,
useful as that may have been
throughout human history.

Remember, instead,
how good it feels
to sit on the front stoop,
close your eyes, feel
the warmth of spring
relieve the tension
in your jaw, as if thawing
some long-hardened part
of your heart.

Unclench your fists—
there is nothing to rage against,

nothing to grasp or resist,
not right this minute.
There is only the unmown lawn,
strewn with weeds and wildflowers
whose names you do not know
and whom you love

nonetheless,
like all of those
anonymous
victims of the virus: imagine
what they would give
to do just this.

THEY HAVE NAMES

All of these dutiful perennials
appearing in the front yard,
unbidden, unannounced,
like so many Samaritans come
to check in, ask if there is anything
to be done
to bolster your spirit,
restore your faith, which, of course,
they already have.

Every petal a prayer answered,
every leaf an affirmation
of life after death, after dark-
ness and desolation, after
despair. The earth repairing
itself as all of us must, making
beauty where there was dust.

They have names, these
emissaries from the underground:
common violet, deadnettle, wild
geranium; primrose, gaywings,
Star of Bethlehem. Bless them.
Say them. Praise them.

GOOD FRIDAY

There has been a terrible misunderstanding
and it has been mine.
This is not what I had planned
when I set out
to identify the essential,
to create something beautiful,
to love and be loved, be good,
avoid doing harm.

I did not intend to make such a mess, so many
bad calls, wrong turns, false starts, one hall
of mirrors leading to another, darker,
more distorted one, until I didn't know
which way was up and couldn't but keep
    moving
forward, opening this door, then that, finding
behind each some horror or delight
or delight that turned out to be horrible.

This isn't the story I wanted to write.
It was supposed to have an elegant arc.
It was supposed to save us from the flood.
It was supposed to have a moral or, at least, a
    point.

My hands smell of cinnamon, cardamom,
nutmeg, and cloves, from kneading dough

for hot cross buns this morning,
half with raisins and walnuts, half without,
for my children who have yet to resign themselves
to taking things as they come, are not yet
    convinced
that our preferences set us up for disappointment,
that we can learn to accept almost any texture,
almost any taste, even come to enjoy
the unexpected sweetness, the unexpected bite.

RESET

First thing in the morning,
pull a jacket over your night dress, slip
bare feet into clogs and carry
the garbage out, its heft the weight
of all the refuse of the week.

Roll the dumpster to the curb, grateful
a bear hasn't gotten there first, not this time.

Notice the air,
cool and fresh as water
from a spring, birdsong like church
bells, or the train whistle
you lay awake listening to
the night before, wondering
where it might be headed and if
you might ride along,
imagining another country,
another century, a grandmother
you never knew, who, too,
must have grown bored,
and tired of her chores,
and dolorous until

something gave her pause,
and she looked around,
and listened,

and felt overcome
by a tenderness toward the new-
born day, how labor affords
its own consolation, its own
euphoric,
            the grass wet with dew,
the paving stones spaced
exactly to match your stride
as you walk back
toward the house,
back into its warmth,
back into your life.

WINDFALL

A budding branch blown down by last night's
    storm
lies on the lawn reminding me of a fawn
my daughter and I came upon on the lake
    road
once, last summer: perfectly intact, its back
dappled like this morning's light through the
    draping
wisteria vines, wet with rain, its eyes closed,
its legs tucked in as if asleep, or in the womb,
though its doe was nowhere to be found,
and she asked, my daughter did, *who made*
    her dead?
And *she won't ever grow up to be a mother?*
    Why will she never
be a mother? And she wept, it seemed, less for
    this
small thing at our feet than for the future
that would not be, this child of three you'd
    think
couldn't see beyond next week, as I can't,
    these days,
our path as indiscernible as that of the wind,
forever turning on a dime, bringing down
    someone
or something that was, just yesterday, alive.

Dear

The mornings are cool here, the light
gray, but it warms throughout the day and,
most afternoons, the sun appears.

At the end of the road, there's a bank
of lilacs in bloom. Out walking,
I smell them as I round the bend
and remember
                    how furious my mother was
when my father uprooted
the bushes around our house
on West Street. I never knew
why, and should ask him, or her,
while I still can, before
the source of every rift becomes
a mystery, and all we know
is that it's there, and permanent,

a scar that never fades and seems,
instead, to darken over time,
though we've forgotten the injury
and how it came to be, the distance
between us growing like the length
of the days, longer and longer until,
before we know it, it's late

evening and we've yet to eat,
yet to call the children in, gather
the laundry from the line, water
the garden, pause

to take a drink from the hose, taste
the mineral bitter-sweet of the well,
as though it were a fountain
that could turn back the hours,
the years, so that we might do it all
over again, more carefully, pay
closer attention.

I hope this finds you holding up,
enjoying the spring where you are,
the return of birds and green and all things
prodigal, prodigious.

Take good care. And love, always.

DOING WITHOUT

I have decided
I can be happy
without happiness.

This desk is enough.
This view
of the wet woods,

a squirrel
balanced
on a branch.

This stillness. This tea.
The sound of my daughter
playing make-believe, distantly.

I do not need
to resolve
our misunderstanding.

I do not need
to feel light
in body or spirit.

I can be
my own
weighted blanket,

comforted
by its heft,
relieved
not to have
to lift it.

ADVANCE DIRECTIVE

My mother tells me
she is putting away
the Hudson Bay blanket
in cedar chips,
for me to keep
when she is gone.

It gets cold
where I live,
and my brother,
farther north,
probably wouldn't
want it.

He is not sentimental
about *things*, though
he feels deeply,
and likely remembers
the heavy ivory wool,
its red and green and black
and yellow stripes,
that followed us
from house to house
to untenable house
when we were
growing up.

I have heard it said
that houses do not so much
pass through our possession
as we through theirs, as if
through the arms of someone
who holds us for a while
and then stays put
when we move on.

I am fond of the scent
of cedar—evergreen,
but distinct from other pines—
evocative of care
having been taken
in hopes of keeping things
in good repair
another year.

THE RADICAL HOSPITALITY OF
THE SENSES

They beckon: the light
on the low bookshelf
at dawn, the sound of mocking-
birds greeting the day,
the smell of bread
toasting, warming the house,
where the morning air feels cool,
and the first sip of water
tastes of kindness.

Notice us, they seem to beg,
come to us, and we will save you
from yourself, that black hole
in your head, where ghost-
thoughts taunt the cowering child.

They promise: you are safe.

They do not deceive you,
even as they dull with age,
blur, fade, still they will bring you
back to the world, where
you belong, gracious
hosts, saying here,
come in, stay. Please,
have a seat, let us

get you a drink, a bite
to eat.

You must be weary,
put up your feet. Tell us
of your journey, we're listening.

LAMENT

I don't remember anyone
ever telling me
how quickly
eyesight fades,
though when
I mention it now,

how, in just these
last weeks, words
have blurred,
it's been confirmed: vision's
precipitous diminishment and,
my mother suggests,
the rest can go
as swiftly: climbing

steps, getting dressed—
the skills we learned as children
and infants disappearing
in reverse: running, jumping,
balance; speech and language;
walking, standing, feeding
ourselves, the pincer grip.

Rolling over, lifting
our heads—everything
but being held, lulled,

kissed on the fontanel,
whispered to
in sing-song tones,
the rhythm of another
heartbeat, then
silence.

INSOMNIA

I read until I think
I'm tired, then trim
the lamp and pull the covers
over my shoulders,
over my head,
curl fetal and begin
counting breaths,
as I have since adolescence,
when the trouble began.

But that's not true:
even as a child
I had a terrible time,
lay awake listening,
as I did last night,
to what must have been
mice scuffling in the attic,
nesting in the fiber-
glass insulation, gnawing,
I imagined, holes
in the woolen clothes
and old photos
stored there.

Back then, what I feared
was someone else
intruding, doing harm,

not myself, my own
gross errors which cannot,
in fact, be feared, only rued,
just as we can't
desire what we have,
dread what has been,
only pine, regret—

conscience the mischief
of mice that keeps us
up nights, and will
not quiet, will
not calm, can, this way,
be counted on.

Motivational

Who am I
to call this
all mistake?

Such arrogance
to assume
culpability,
such cowardice
to deny it.

So simple-
minded: the desire
to decide
if fault is ours
or beyond our power.

Either way,
we are here,
and best
get on with it—

what's done
is done, and what
isn't isn't.

AND MIRRORS

The woods behind
our house are thick
with oak and maple,
beech and hickory.

Once, I wanted to live
in the city.

For Mother's Day, my son
dug a fire pit out back. We had
our first the other night—roasted
marshmallows, whittled sticks.

All evening, the smoke
kept shifting, drifting
in different directions.

I could feel my eyes
grow narrow, my expression
blank as I stared into the flames.

The little one swung
from a rope swing,
high into the trees,
shrieking with glee.

I hope she'll remember
the cringe of burnt sugar,
whiff of singed hemlock.
I hope she'll forget
the look on my face.

Belle-Mère

Surely she wasn't
always wicked. Young,
and beautiful if only
because she was young,
the first time, she married
for love.

The second, she wed
to secure her children's
futures, she claimed,
as though she could.

Can you blame her? No
matter, she was again
left destitute, and
it was then she became
bitter and, yes, cynical:

sweetness and innocence
cloying reminders
of a former self,
one who had hoped to shape
a redemptive narrative, her own
happily-ever-after, one
who had hoped.

MIDSUMMER IN THE
MOUNTAINS

Every morning,
before it's too hot,
my son and I walk
a three-mile loop
around our neighborhood,
first down through a ravine, then
up & out of it, past a park
and playing fields,
along a lake and,
not long before we're finished,
into the shade
of a bamboo grove,
where it always feels cooler,
as though the leaves were emitting
a mist of their own.

Each day, this pleases me:
the heat we generate
and the brief relief of it
as we round that bend, the end
not quite in sight, but near enough
for a small reprieve to see us
through the last steep rise,
the final push prior
to arriving
home.

TRUTH AND RECONCILIATION

We packed a picnic, drove
south along the Blue Ridge
Parkway to Mount Pisgah,
found a table in dappled shade,
laid it with a runner
made from the curtains
she and my father had hung
in their first apartment
in Detroit, circa 1968.

Cloth napkins, mason jars,
China plates—yet we ate
dill pickles and sandwiches,
potato chips and dip, as if
we were still girls, speaking
of whether or not we believed
in anything anymore, if
there was any such thing
as an incontrovertible truth,
what we might have done differently,
if it might have made a difference—

There was white oleander
in the background, thunder
in the distance. I said that, for me,
it wasn't about belief
so much as *acting*
as though certain things were so.

Such as: it couldn't have been
otherwise. Such as: some things
are beyond our control. If only
to forgive one another; if only
to disburden ourselves.

EXIT STRATEGY

Most mornings, soon
after the sun comes up,
I feed the cat and brush my teeth,
make tea and climb back into bed,
let the warmth of the sheets ease
what is aching.

Through the open window
comes the thrum of insects,
trill of chickadees, a little light,
cool air of mid-September.

From the lamp, a dim
glow. From the other room,
my daughter in her white night-
dress, half asleep.

She slips under the covers
beside me, smiles silently,
as if speech might break
the spell cast by quiet,
the remnants of dream.

Wanting this part of the day
to open like a portal, take us in,
expand without end.

Part II

What Is Taken

After Hoagland's Field Guide

Once, on a path around the backside of
    Beaver Lake,
I saw a rabbit cowering in the bramble, barely
    visible,
its tweed coat almost indistinguishable from
    the winter grass.

And I took your arm
to slow you down,
and point it out, without a sound.

Then the three of us were all
motionless, our eyes locked, wondering,
perhaps, who would make the next move,
away or toward, who might hurt whom.

But the cold was too much, the sky
too gray to pause for long, and so we trudged on
through the mud, leaving that small, wild thing
to fend for itself, as all of us must.

And we kept talking
ourselves into that hole of unknowns, joking
caustically to warm up, and diffuse
the tension of everything that is
forever at stake, distract ourselves

from the wind's leather strap, lashing us
for the hubris of being here at all.

And the lake's surface cracked and refracted
like so much thin ice, and we went back
to your place and ate and drank and danced
and fucked.

And none of it mattered. Not much.

ALL SHE KNOWS

after Stephen Dobyns

These are the last days of winter.
The morning air smells of turned earth,
while the sound of birds in the garden
is like a stirring in the heart, the desire
to open a gate and walk through it.

A woman alone descends her front steps,
turns left and begins at a clip, the wind
in her face an antidote to impatience, a way
of going out to greet the season,
rather than waiting for it to come to her,
as she would have, once, not wanting
to rush what wasn't ready to arrive
of its own volition, imagining spring
a shy creature that couldn't be coaxed.

But what good has that done her, really?
Here she is, nearing fifty, and still
uncertain of everything.

All she knows is today
is slightly warmer than the day before,
slightly lighter later.

And there are the beginnings
of buds on some branches, green nubs

thrusting up through the dirt. The hurt
she has felt for so long isn't going anywhere,
but she is, God help her, if only
around the block, not to take stock
of her thoughts, but to shed them,
like layers of wool she's worn for too long.

She imagines them strewn
on the neighbors' lawns, cast off
as if on her way to a swimming hole
where she will plunge headlong
into the swirling eddies, a girl again,
without a care in the whirl,
weightless as the nymphs that danced
upon the surface of the rivers
of her innocence.

WANT

These strawberries want
brown sugar, maple syrup,
want to be dipped
and brought to your lips
still dripping with the water
in which they were rinsed,

want to leave
pink juice on your fingertips
so that you can't
but lick them clean,
want to be sweeter
than they seem.

Maybe they didn't get
that slightly sandy, slightly acidic
soil that might have made them so,
maybe they just didn't have enough
time to grow ripe
before being picked?

In any case, they are here now,
in this shallow white bowl, red
and slick and prettier
to look at than to taste
were you here
to taste them.

ORNITHOLOGY

I think now they were swallows,
not swifts, dipping and diving
above the lake the other evening,
their iridescence invisible
in the dusk.

Every afternoon, I come home
to wreckage in the kitchen,
my two teen-aged sons
having been left
to fend for themselves
for too long.
                    One
rarely gets out of bed, says
he hates it here, hates being
alive, finds consciousness
unbearable, apologizes, can't
wait to be gone.

The other hates me
for asking him to do the dishes,
brings me butter lettuce, young
kale he's grown from seed
and I make a dressing
of olive oil, lemon,
Dijon and salt,
toss in some pistachios,
avocado, grape tomatoes.

I could forgive them
anything if not they me.

My small daughter wants
ice cream, wears a butterfly
mask, pretends she has wings,
flitting and fluttering up
and down the sidewalk, calling out
the colors of flowers.

A message from the vet says
their records indicate our cat
is due for his rabies shot,
and I wonder how it is
their records don't also indicate
he was euthanized there, last month.

All of this makes me
want to call my father, makes me
want to be held, makes me
want a drink, though I had too much
the other night and so
know I shouldn't, know instead
to swallow hard, walk
back to the lake, watch
the birds again and think on
what has hatched, what
they're so hungry for, what
they, in fact, are.

METEOROLOGY

Each morning, I check the forecast
to see how cold it got in the night, what
the temperature is now, how
cold it will be when we
stand in front of the school, clutching
our mugs of tea or coffee, shifting
from foot to foot, waiting
to help the sleepy children
out of their car seats, into their backpacks, say
goodbye to their parents and walk them
through the doors and down the hall.

How cold will it be when we take them
out to the playground? Will they need
jackets, mittens, hats; will it be warm enough
for them to shed their coats, tuck them
by hood or sleeve through the chain link
    fence,
a sort of ornament, like those that form the
    makeshift
shrines that bloom where someone's died.

And how cool will it be after
work, when I walk around the lake,
will the sun have come out, stayed out,
will I need sunscreen, when will it set?

And later in the week? Rain, a chance
of frost, a warming trend?
Today, strong winds, the temperature due
to drop by afternoon, so I resolve
to bundle, layer, do what I can
to be comfortable outside regardless.

It's what I've learned after years of failing:
to dress for the weather, be easy
with the coming and the going,
do not pretend the cold can be wished
away, the sun wished back, any more than
love.

Even still, it must be said, I also check
the forecast where you've gone.

SATURDAY, MID-SPRING AND RAIN

So I start laundry, set my daughter up
to paint at the dining room table, fry
potatoes and onions for lunch, bake
cookies while her brothers watch a movie.

When the rain stops, we go out and turn
the last of our raised beds, sow seeds
she chose weeks ago and has
been eager to plant—blue boy
bachelor's buttons, zinnia, chamomile—
such pretty pictures on the packets,
though I tell her we can't be sure
which will actually take.

Before dinner, I walk
to the lake, where the dog-
wood blossoms are at their peak,
and an enormous osprey
is putting on a show, sky-
dancing, I've heard it called,
then plunging feet-first
to seize what he's seen,
screeching as he emerges,
a fish athrash in his talons.

In bed, I read to her
from *The Chamber of Secrets*, then
to myself a piece on field guides,
how what begins with naming
becomes about relationship,
attention the beginning
of devotion.

And the end? I cannot fathom.

MINOR BLUES

I can't listen to gypsy jazz, as I did
the other night, without thinking
of Paris, and of Woody
Allen, who used to be
all about Gershwin and New York,
but seems to have become
more Gallic as he's aged,
more romantic and even more
morally suspect, though I don't know
that it's him so much as the times
that have changed.

What was once
ignored or indulged now
condemned and disdained,
which is probably why I feel
a little guilty for enjoying it,
the bouncing swing, the relentless
strumming, the sense
of forward motion, of not just *being*
but *becoming*, as I was
all those years ago:

Twenty and living
in Montmartre, climbing each day
the steps to Sacred Heart, looking
out over rooftops and chimneys, the maze

of winding streets, as if they were mine
for the taking, then descending
into Pigalle, where I was sometimes mistaken
for a prostitute, by Jehovah's Witnesses,
    especially,
who tried to save me even there.

But I did not want to be saved; I wanted
to be ravaged, as only someone
who had not been could.

But that's not true:
I still do, which must be why
I can't stop loving
the guitar and bass, the violin,
the taste of gin, the urge to dance,
to lead and be led
into temptation.

The Pleasure of Remembering

Not until I am home alone,
nearly a week later,
do I allow myself
the pleasure of remembering
the peaches we ate
on the riverbank
where we pulled the canoe ashore
and dove in, the stones
you skipped and I
failed to skip, your dog
leaping and bouncing
like a lamb amid the bramble,
gleeful as we were.

Traveling along the parkway
through Shenandoah,
in no particular hurry,
we pulled off at one lookout
after another, each a feast
spread before us,
peregrines nesting
nearby, their young
newly fledged.

Midday, we took a path
through the woods, found a log
and ate leftovers, before continuing

onto your childhood home, perched
on another river, states away, where,
the next day, we floated twice,
sunning ourselves on the dock in between,
staring up at the sky, our feet dangling
in the cool water, still
astonished by the fox
we'd seen in passing.

Meadowlands

When in doubt, there is never
any shortage of mistakes
to write about. In this case: wild
raspberries and their countless
cousins—salmon, bramble,
thimble, wine, cloud—one of which
we found on the way down
from the lookout at Pyramid Point,
that cold, overcast afternoon
in Michigan, mid-July, when we decided
to take another path
that quickly narrowed, turned
steep, and my kids insisted
we double back.

I couldn't blame them,
having taken them
down so many wrong roads before,
and yet, when we came to a fork
and had to choose
between returning to the trailhead
or heading for the meadow,
they agreed, and we proceeded,
not knowing where we were
going, but intrigued
by the prospect of a clearing
which we had to believe must be

just around the next bend, even when
it wasn't, one of them running ahead
to check, report back: still nothing,
nothing yet.
       And then,
when the youngest claimed
she couldn't take another step
and shlumped down, crying, hugging
her knees, her brother
took her hand, and coaxed her,
taking up the mantle as we do
when another's despair exceeds
our own.
       And there it was:
a lake of tall grass spread before us,
and no one thinking yet
about how we would find our way
home, or what this fruit was called,
just taking it in, tasting it, letting
the sweet red break on our tongues.

TO REMEMBER YOU'RE ALIVE

after Jim Harrison

To remember you're alive, take a walk
in the rain with a married man,
another poet, your close friend,
while your own love is far,
your children asleep
in their beds, through the town
where you were married
a quarter century before.
                              Gaze
into the fog
hovering over the lake,
its surface shivering
when the rain touches it,
an eagle with a fish lifting off,
a lone duck drifting.
                    Sit
under the picnic shelter
talk of books, frustrations, aging—
your parents', your own, your children's
coming-of-age, the ache of it.
Let his devotion make you
admire him more.

When you say goodbye,
embrace, linger, feel
his lips graze your cheek,
yours his.

Drive home listening
to a Scottish ballad
on the classical station,
Joy for the One You Love.

Don't speed. Focus
on the road. Know that,
at any moment, one
of the semis barreling toward you
could hydroplane, lose control.

When you get back, make pancakes,
eggs. Sip black coffee, lick
syrup from your fingertips, send
your love a flare, tell him
you can't wait for his return.

Translation

For *admire*, read *desire*.
For *remember, forget*.
For *alive*, read *mortal*.
For *take a walk*, read *go to bed*.

For *gaze*, read *dive*.
For *fog, mist*.
For *hovering over, emerging from*.

For *lake*, read *my body*.
For *the rain, yours*.
For *eagle, spirit*.
For *duck, heart*.

For *drifting*, read *swelling*.
For *sit*, read *lie down*.
For *picnic shelter, ghost elms*,
a hundred years gone.

For *talk*, read *touch*.
For *books*, read *breasts*.
For *frustrations, shoulders*.
For *aging, back*.

For *ache*, read *ache*.

For *say goodbye*, read *stay*.
For *drive home, stay*.

For *focus, imagine*.
For *road, a field*.

For *know*, read *believe*.
For *could*, read *won't*.

For *get back*, read *wake*.
For *pancakes, love*.

For *sip, drink*.
For *coffee, wine*.
For *syrup, honey*.
For *your, my*.

WHAT HAPPENED

What happened, happened once.

We met on a Thursday, but that doesn't matter.
It was early, the parking lot empty.
You brought bagels. I broke off a piece of one
and put the rest in my coat pocket.

There had been thunderstorms in the night.
It was raining gently still. The path was narrow
and wound through the trees—hemlocks,
    mostly—
and you asked how I had come to poetry,
and I asked you the same, and we talked of that
as we walked through the woods toward the
    lake,
stopping to admire a large toad near a stump,
various mushrooms. And when we came to
    where
the trees gave way
to sand and dune grass,
we stared out at the water in silence until you
    said
let's not go yet, and we walked down from that
    first rise
and up to the top of the next, the sand shifting
beneath our feet, making your bad ankle ache.

And you asked if you could hold me,
and we pressed our bodies against one another
and stayed there, our hands passing over each
    other's
hips and backs, and I took off my jacket
so that there would be less between us,
so that we could be closer, though we
    couldn't, really.
And you looked down the front of my blouse
    and said
you'd always been curious and, a little later,
    asked
if I would mind if we stopped.
And we walked back
into the woods and kept talking, though I
    can't remember now
of what. There was a chipmunk, and twice big
    branches
crashed through the trees to the ground not
    far from us,
and you took my hand and said you'd always
    thought
our bodies would be well matched, and they
    were.

Undressing the Muse

When do our senses know any thing so utterly as
when we lack it? —Marilynne Robinson

Whatever you do, don't
be overwhelmed. Or,
be overwhelmed. Why not?

To the best of my knowledge,
no one has ever died of desire.
Its consequences, maybe, but not
desire itself.
                A wish or a want,
no matter how urgent, is not
the absence of food or water,
clothing or shelter. It is not air,
nor love, nor loving, even.
                              It is not
something we can't live without,
nor something we can't live with.

It is not poison; it is not a bullet
or a knife. It is not madness, exactly.

It is like hunger, but it is not
starvation.
                And sex
poems are not sex, so why not
swerve away?

The imagination promises
no one anything. The imagination cannot
make promises and therefore
cannot be unfaithful any more
than the wind can be
unfaithful.

Our minds may be
the masters of our bodies, but
the imagination has a mind
of its own.

Just look at it:
undressing us, shamelessly, in that
stark room full of natural light. Letting
the strap slip from my shoulder, my dress
fall to the floor.

Pulling your pullover over
your head, unbuttoning your button-down,
unbuckling your belt.
Pushing you
back against the wall. Bringing me
to my knees.

River Vigil

1

You have gone
back to where you came from,
greeted the water, your mother,
she who will take you
to where you'll put in,
leave you to launch
while I wait for you, here.

2

In the first picture you send,
the sky looks clear, the sun
glinting off the river's glass,
though you report a storm
in the night, thunder, the water
rising.

3

I look up Hancock, New York,
see it's named for the famed
signatory, study the second snapshot:
your dog perched like a figurehead
at the prow of the canoe
and I envy her
her proximity to you.

4

And so I stop pretending
this isn't about love.

5

In your absence, I eat
tomato sandwiches.
It is August, after all,
and they are ripe
for the picking,
sunset-striped, gold
and vermillion, beginning
to split from within
with their own becoming.

Good bread, mayonnaise,
basil, flake salt.

6
My son sees a man
hiding in the shrubs
across the street
from our house.

We close windows,
lock doors, turn off
lights. Lie awake
listening, frightened.

This is one part
I don't like
about living
alone.

7

In the morning, no word.
I imagine you waking,
the scent of the tent,
cool air, coffee, river-water
cupped in your hands,
splashed on your face,
last night's small fire
still smoldering.

8

But that may be me,
adding. More likely,
it's the dog in your face,
asking to be let out,
and you, too,
relieving yourself,
as you do in the morning
before returning to bed,
nudging me, asking
without asking
to be let in.

9

I listen to an old
interview from before
I knew you, hear
in your voice
something I have
not heard before:
The before life—
before the stroke, your
separation, the pandemic, me.

10

Countless eagles
where you've been. Here,
a single cormorant,
a solitary heron.

You say you like
the mergansers best,
their rust-colored heads,
but also the long-legged
shore birds, and I imagine

wrapping mine around you,
straddling you on a park bench
as I sometimes do
for the pleasure
of the expression
it brings to your face—

part surprise, part
embarrassment, part
gratitude, part arousal.

11

By today, you should be
halfway: a hundred miles
behind you, a hundred
to go, but in your silence
I imagine a run-in with that bear
under the bridge, rocks and current,
unrelenting heat, and I storm
out of my house
to walk around the lake
despite distant lightning,
gathering clouds.

12

You are down
to your last beer,
and I my last tomato,
though I have to believe
there will be more
to come, if only
we are patient.

EARLY OUT ON BEAVER LAKE

The sycamores, philanthropists
in late life, let go
their bronze and copper coins
along the path.

The lake lies
perfectly still, a lover
in wait of light, reflecting
rowboats' painted hulls, belly-
up on the grassy bank, the dog-
woods' muted maroons
and greens, suggesting
symmetries everywhere,
or the illusion of them—
the entire scene a Rorschach test
to determine what might be made
of a given day, what wasted.

Canada geese camouflaged in autumn
fog—a flannel cloak the morning wears,
then casts off when the sun appears—
call and respond in a native tongue
I do not speak but sometimes think
I apprehend. (*Where are you*? *I am here.*
Are we safe? *Who knows, who knows*?)

OCTOBER 24TH

Autumn's auburns
and umbers
have long been sung,
but what strikes me
today, out walking
around the lake again,
is the unabashed azure
of the October sky—
so unlike summer's
over-simplified cerulean.

Akin, instead,
to love later in life,
or water: darker,
deeper,
yet no less clear,
and all the more
astonishing.

AFTER MONTHS AWAY

My oldest son comes home,
hugs me hard,
feels solid in my arms.

Takes his little sister in his
and swings her around,
both of them laughing.

We have hard cider to celebrate.
I've made chili, and they carve
a pumpkin together, reaching in
with their bare hands
to pull out the stringy pulp,
as he so loved to as a kid
he once declared that's what
he'd do when he grew up:
become a professional
pumpkin-carver, certain
that must be a thing,
as he has been of nothing since.

With a serving spoon, they scrape
clean the inner walls, and I sort the seeds,
rinse and salt and set them to roast,
their aroma filling the house.

My younger son, taller
than his brother now, joins in.
They wrestle and carouse
like the bear cubs they are,
the punches they pull
a form of love.

When the face is finished,
I carry it out to the porch
in the dark, light a votive
and watch its eyes light up,
its crooked grin
aglow from within.

A cold wind
plays the chimes, rustles
the last dry leaves on the trees.
And the candle flickers
but does not go out.

November 11th

Once a week or so, when we've dropped
her brother at the gym, and if there are
no pressing errands to be run, I take
my daughter on a date—a flight
of kombucha at Rosetta's kitchen,
sushi at a sidewalk café, doughnuts
at Vortex or, her favorite, avocado
toast at the City Bakery.

A window seat if one's available.
Coffee for me, bubbly water
for her, and no one and nothing
to compete for our attention.

I try not to look at my phone, try
to answer her questions
such as today's about alfalfa
sprouts and Veteran's Day,
the things that remain
mysteries to six-year-olds—

And to me, hard pressed as I am
to explain war, or why
her grandfather would never want
to be thanked for his service
in Vietnam, how often we don't
know what we're getting into

until it's too late, then find ourselves
having done something
we can't undo, and hate.

All the while, she keeps
taking bites, her eyes wide
and glistening, as his must have been,
then, before I knew him,
the tangle of tiny shoots
the Arabs called the father
of all foods
curled into a small nest
on the side of her plate.

THE ART OF SIMPLE FOOD

The art of aioli, almonds, and anise biscotti.
The art of basil and béchamel.
The art of beets, Belgian endive, and berries.
The art of biscuits and blueberry pie.
The art of bread, broth, and Brussels sprouts.
The art of buckwheat and buttermilk.
The art of capers, caponata, and cauliflower.
The art of chard, chilies, chocolate, and
    chowder.
The art of cobblers and colanders.
The art of crepes, croutons, currants, and
    cutting boards.
The art of earthenware and eggplant.
The art of farro and fennel.
The art of garlic, gazpacho, and gougères.
The art of grains, grapefruit, and gratins.
The art of greens and gremolata.
The art of harissa and hummus.
The art of ice cream.
The art of kale and kumquats.
The art of leeks, lemon, and lentils.
The art of mortars and pestles.
The art of omelets, onions, and oranges.
The art of parsnips and pasta.
The art of peaches, pears, and peppercorns.
The art of peppers, persimmons, and pesto.

The art of polenta, pomegranate, and
     pumpkin.
The art of radicchio, raspberries, and
     ratatouille.
The art of ravioli, risotto, and roasting.
The art of rocket and rutabaga.
The art of sauteeing and scones.
The art of semolina, shallots, and shortcake.
The art of sieves, simmering, soda bread, and
     soup.
The art of strawberries and sugar.
The art of sushi and sweet potatoes.
The art of tabbouleh, tangerines, tapenade,
     and tarts.
The art of tomatoes, truffles, and turnips.
The art of vanilla and vinaigrettes.
The art of waffles, walnuts, and wine.
The art of yams and yeast.
The art of alliteration.
The art of invoking, with words,
what we love, what we long for,
what we miss, what brought us
pleasure, brought us
together at a table—set with flowers,
lit with candles—what might take us
back—

to when we were happiest, to when
we were most whole,
to that we might be once
again.

Part III

What Is Left

DECEMBER 1ST

Frost on the grass; I can see
my breath. Bundled against the cold,
I move to outpace it.

Overhead, crows crisscross and caw—
the sky gray-blue, gray-pink, gray-
lavender, the sun about to rise
above the mountains,
through the clouds.

Fog hovers
over the lake
and the lake reflects
the all of it:

Geese I thought were gone
remain, bedded down
on the barren bank. My parents,
ill but alive, my children lost but still
wandering the face of the earth, and so
all hope isn't.

And I am thinking
of last weekend,
the pleasure of being
naked in bed with you—
flannel sheets, candlelight,

a little music, something to sip—
how I'd crawl on hands and knees
to be there again.

In the bare trees, the sparrows'
careful nests appear abandoned,
but one stand of dogwoods
has yet to lose its leaves.
On the far shore they blaze,
a fire in the hearth of my heart.

Waiting

Snow overnight, its glare mimicking
daylight before dawn, silhouettes
of evergreens leaning in the wind,
their boughs laden. Chimes
on the front porch playing,
blue shadows everywhere.

In the quiet, I make
muffins for breakfast,
read your manuscript
while they bake, picture you
on the river last summer—
your hands, the paddle, pulling—
the distance between us
lessening with every stroke,
as though you were making
your way to me, as though
you had been since you were born: one
long, meandering course
through childhood and work,
marriage and divorce,
near-death and loss and life—all
to bring you to where
I have been waiting,
though I didn't know I was waiting
and you didn't know I was waiting

and we still don't know exactly
where we will go from here.

I dream a garden, a creek, a path
through a sea of ferns, good food
to eat, books to read, love to make—
in the morning, and in the afternoon,
and on nights like the one to come:
the world outside frozen
as the past is frozen: cold and hard
and unforgiving; but inside
the future soft and warm and now

I take the muffins from the oven,
pull one apart, inhale its steam
fragrant with August blueberries,
the snow still coming down.

HALF PAST FEBRUARY

Not even winters last as long as they used to.
Do you remember how interminable they
    once seemed?
Snow for months and gray and cold. The sadness
that set in. There no longer seems time to get
    good and despondent,
already signs of spring again. I would take the
    doldrums
and melancholy back just to slow things
    down a bit.
The thought that it will all be over before we
    know it
infinitely heavier on my heart than the
    harshest season of our history.

GETTING BY

I have chopped pistachios
leftover from a wedding
cake I made last month,
arugula from yesterday's salad,
lemons for the cold
I've been fighting,
                and I am
trying to remember the recipe
for the Sicilian spaghetti
my mother made for me once
when she came to visit
my apartment on Chestnut Street,
the one in the Jefferson Building,
red brick with arched windows,
flower boxes, which used to be
some sort of institution,
where I lived for six months,
between men who had begged me
to come, then insisted I go.

It had a little terrace
with French doors that opened
out onto a church
parking lot with a view
of a cross that glowed
in the night like certain
thoughts that kept me up.

It had red pepper flakes
and lots of olive oil, tasted bright
and bitter and is
what I'm craving now, because
it is what can be
made with the ingredients
on hand.

RECOVERY

Mid-February, and the temperature reaches
sixty for the first time in months.
After school it is light late
enough for my daughter and me
to go out to the garden, examine
the damage wrought by winter
and neglect—hydrangeas dried in bloom
and never pruned, already budding;
bamboo taking root in the raised beds
where overgrown mums have become
tangled in the netting meant to keep
something or other out, dead annuals
and weeds we can't distinguish
from what little there is that might return.

I think I recognize the leaves
of a strawberry plant, the smell
of mint, a thatch of thyme that might
recover if I cut it back. She says
the fence could use a coat of paint, says
next time, let's take better care
of our yard, our house, already aware
of the impermanence of this one, and I ask,
but what about here? Why not now?

It is never too late or it always is. It is *the same
difference*, though even as a girl I bristled

at that expression, the implication
that it doesn't matter, isn't worth the effort
to parse, to consider more carefully
what may or may not be
beyond repair, rake out the beds
where dark green tips of daffodils
struggle upward, refuse to be buried
alive, salvage what we can.

A WEEKEND

It was, by all accounts, too perfect for a poem,
too lacking in darkness and pathos. For twenty-
four hours, I scarcely thought of the imminent
deaths of those I love, strangers, war.

It had been a year since we met,
and we were returning to the scene:
the farmer's market where we foraged
wild mushrooms for a risotto
we would make that evening, asparagus
shoots slim as the stems of flowers.

The café where we sat outside, sipping
cappuccinos once again, then a long walk
through the woods—forest bathing,
some call it—warmer than it had been
the year before, on the spring equinox,
the trees still leafless, sunlight raining
down on my shoulders and arms, bare
for the first time in months.

A flight at a brewery overlooking
a valley, mountains in the distance,
the smell of wood chips, thawing—
Barn Flower Blond, Elder Fairy, Goat's Eye,
something Belgian—and a bite before

heading home for naptime—our favorite
euphemism for love in the afternoon.

We spread a blanket in the grass
of your secret garden, secluded
by shrubbery, brought books and dark
chocolate (with, it must be said, a luscious
strawberry filling), a pillow to share—
and lay among the newly blooming
crocuses, a sea of purple petals, orange
tongues of flame, birdsong, our faces
framed by the blue of the sky by turns.

Afterward, we opened a bottle of Prosecco,
cold and crisp and quenching. You stirred
stock into the glistening rice, while I stripped
fresh herbs from their stalks. As I said, it was
far too lovely for a poem, and yet it was.

FROM HERE

I don't know when
I will see you again
but it won't be
soon enough. Likely
spring will have passed
with its pale greens
and newness, its buds
and soft air. Likely
summer will have come,
thrumming and insistent,
neither of our favorite
times of year.

But I will take
what I can get.

We are all
at the mercy
of the calendar, the clock,
the current carrying us
forward in its blue blur.

This morning, I woke
and forgot for a moment
you would not be beside me
when I opened my eyes,

how far away you are
now.

On our walk this afternoon,
Mara picked two dandelions
gone to seed, gave me one
and told me to make a wish.

This world needs
so many things,
but all I want is for you
to survive another season.

There must be a way
to get there from here.

You Know, You Don't Have to Keep It

I'm told, of the kitten we found
last weekend, out walking
along a country road in the rain,
crying out from the bramble
so dense we could see nothing
at first, and started to walk away.

But her plea became louder,
more desperate, and so
you found a fallen branch
and I bushwhacked
through the thicket until
I could just make out
a tiny face amid the thorns,
pulled my hood around my head,
my sleeve over my hand, reached in
and grasped her, wet
and trembling as all of us have been,
tucked her in to the top of my overalls
and carried her to the lodge where she licked
milk from my fingertip, warmed
and transformed into a ball of fluff,
coming back to life
when she could easily have not.

Later, we returned to the scene
to make sure there weren't others,
a mother, but, finding nothing
and no one, knew then
she would be ours—not to possess,
but to care for as we can't not
the lives that have befallen us.

WHAT REDEEMS THE WHOLE

My house is full of clutter;
I have not been successful
in work or love, my children
are at risk and my body
is aging, losing shape.

But, I tell myself, I can still be happy
if I just focus
on the luminous particulars:
cool air of morning, birdsong,
my daughter's braids.

And yet, the clutter—
the clutter makes it difficult
to distinguish axis of beauty
from the general dim and din,
so I think maybe I'll pack away
the winter jackets, see if that
won't help, take out the dead
flowers, freshen the water
for those that remain,
cull the clothes in my closet
of all synthetics, even the shimmery
dress Sally gave me
before dying while we
were still young and lithe,
riding our bicycles in tall boots

and short skirts up and down
the city streets.

Yes, maybe
if I wear only linen, second hand,
I can feel noble
and elegant in my simplicity,
like an Eileen Fisher ad but less
expensive, as I try to feel
by telling myself that teaching
preschool is a real and honorable profession,
not some made-up entrepreneurial effort
like those that have made my friends
and nemeses rich, and that my children,
however troubled, have expanded my heart
immeasurably, and that the love I am
now in, however new, could last, could be
what redeems the whole
long muddled narrative,
as might God, or poetry,
if we could believe.

NEVER AGAIN

How many summers
have I made the trip home
to Northern Michigan?
Twenty-some, I would guess,
from whichever end-of-the-earth
I had taken up residence,
with whichever children
or partner or lover I had
or without when I was without.

I might have bought a house
with what it cost to get there
and back and stay and eat.
I might have written a book
with the time it took and yet
I went, mostly to sit
on my dad's back deck,
sip black coffee and watch
the birds come to his feeders,
the kids running around
the yard until they were
no longer kids but grown
men, tossing a football
into the sky that stayed
light late into the night
before filling with bats
and stars which meant

it was time for a fire, its blaze
illuminating all of our faces
as we sat around and talked
and laughed and drank
a beer, year after year after
year after year, for fear
one would be the last.

This past, my father
made the trek with us
around North Bar Lake
to Lake Michigan,
in the heat of the beating
sun, his whole body aching,
a shock of pain from
his bad leg with every step.

He clenched his teeth
and bore it, and when
the open water came
into view, he said *hallelujah,*
it was worth it, and
never again.

YOUR STORAGE IS ALMOST FULL

You do not have enough
memory to upload
new photos, I'm told,
when I try and fail
and fail again.

Would I like to go to settings
and review large attachments,
I'm asked, and comply.

There I see my daughter,
dancing in a white dress
to "Black Magic Woman"
at a neighborhood picnic,
a high school classmate singing
"Landslide" at a barn dance,
a child chanting "All the Colors
of the Rainbow" at a kirtan
at the local yoga studio, a bear
ambling down the middle
of Gracelyn Avenue, my mother
smiling, kissing the crown
of a baby's head.

How to choose
between these, and my son's
marching band, playing

the halftime show at a football game
last night, my daughter imitating
the cheerleaders in the stands,
the butterfly that landed
on my hand on the playground
yesterday afternoon, its iridescent wings
patterned with orange and blue and you
and me standing atop yet another mountain,
before yet another waterfall, yet again
happy to be where we are, so happy we can't
but try to stop time, capture an image,
a memento, anything that won't be
erased, taken from us.

How Persimmons

A dear friend is painting
the door of her studio-to-be,
a room of her own
at long last, after years
of endless longing.

It is laid out on sawhorses,
the door, a deep persimmon
that will require several coats.
She sends a snapshot
of her work in progress,
brush in hand,
and I am reminded
of another friend,
how persimmons
were among the last
foods she could stomach,
overripe and abundant
on a neighbor's tree,
unwanted by anyone else, but she
could not get enough of them,
their pulpy sweetness,
their taut skin, something
that did not make her sick
when everything else did.

I took her bowl after bowlful,
left them outside her door
not wanting to wake her,
not wanting to find her
already gone, as she is now,
unlike us, who must keep calling
our desires into existence,
their colors rich, and vivid,
and saturated.

I REMEMBER

By the end of October,
the leaves were at their peak,
Kimberly Avenue
a tunnel of gold,
and I strolled with you
in your pram
past the grand houses
I could not imagine
inhabiting,
and we paused
to pet passing dogs,
and you could not
yet talk but knew
to let them sniff
your fingertips
before gently stroking
the fur between their ears
and you knew no fear
and little loss
and even then
I wished
that I could protect you
from all that was to come,
though I myself
did not yet know
what that was.

FORGIVENESS

The sun is bright, the air is crisp,
the trees let fly their tattered flags.
I stare into their flashing flames
and blame no one for anything.

DISMANTLING CHRISTMAS

It was just five days
after Twelfth Night
when I finally disassembled
the Christmas tree.

The family who'd come
to celebrate long gone,
I worked alone, laying to rest
decades-worth of ornaments
in bins where they're kept
in the dark between seasons—
blown glass and wool and straw,
a hundred-year-old peanut shell
bedecked with crepe paper streamers,
my grandfather's as a child.

Then the wooden cranberries,
Italian lights, the handknit tree skirt
I shook off the front porch
before carrying the small,
brittle-branched fir to a corner
of the yard where, I hoped,
birds might shelter before it's burned
in a bonfire come summer.

Which is when I noticed the car
parked in the lot across the street,

its doors flung open despite the cold,
its stereo blaring while one
shadowy figure paced back and forth,
enacting some ritual
I could not comprehend.

And so I went inside
and locked the doors,
and dimmed the lights,
and watched through the stand
of cypress as I hoped no
one was watching me.

And I climbed into bed and listened hard
for my son's key in the door,
as once he might have strained to hear
sleigh bells on the roof, half-afraid
he would, half-afraid he wouldn't.

CADMIUM

In the backyard, forsythia
blooming, though I've not
set foot there in weeks.
Showering, I see them
through the bathroom window,
a shower of yellow
the color of a favorite dress
my daughter wears and wearing
makes me aware she will
outgrow it soon.

           The color, too,
of popcorn orchids at Oku,
that Japanese curry house we went to
a few times in Honolulu,
many moons ago,
and of the Happiness Soup
I used to make and then stopped
making with the glut of summer
squash in Charleston, the golden disks
like so many infant suns my sons
would not so much as touch.

           Out walking
in the sun: dogwood blossoms,
daffodils, dandelions and violets
dotting neighbors' lawns; azaleas,
crocuses—the list goes on and on
but just now

it is the forsythia that strikes me
like a Zen master's lash: notice this
before it's gone.

ALMOST

I am leafing through
a book of poems, looking
for one I might send
to you. I know this is not
how we are supposed to read—
seeking, solicitous—but I am
hoping to be stunned
by an image, able
to astound you in turn,
make you blush with desire
as you did just last night,
though it was dark
and I could not see
your face but felt
its warmth on my back, sensed
your hunger—predatory, almost,
but tender, as you took me
from behind, like the animals
we used to be
who hunted reverently,
made use of every inch
of fur and flesh—

It is our anniversary,
the Persian New Year.
On my way to work,
long before dawn,

I hear a piece on NPR
about the traditional way
of making yogurt, wrapping
bowls of milk in blankets,
letting them rest until they've coddled
perfectly, the whey reserved
and added to cakes
that will taste of its tang—
almost lemony, almost
like spring's first sun—
subtle, butter-yellow,
stunning.

WALKING

The sky, a mottled gray.
Cold, light rain, and it seemed
later than it was, almost dark.

The blossoms—redbud,
dogwood, ragwort—
brighter by contrast,
brighter than when bathed
in morning light.

For the first time that day,
I paused,
breathed the ozone,
green growing things,
and in that moment,
I was no longer
over living.

I walked on in a fog, unsure
where I was going,
one foot in front of the other until
I'd almost come full circle,
then came a break
in the clouds.
                Behind me,
yet I could see
everything illuminated

and turned around
to glimpse the sun
sending down shafts
like a ladder out
just before it set.

Hikmet wrote: *we must live
as if we will never die.* Too,
we must do whatever it is
that makes us not want to.

AGAIN, MY DAUGHTER ASKS ME TO PLAY

And I say we can take a walk,
make dinner, clean out her closet
or paint, water the thirsty
plants in the garden.

She means with dolls,
stuffed animals, maybe
a board game. It is a common
impasse: my inability against
her need. Or: my reluctance,
her desire.

As a compromise, I suggest
a deck of conversation cards,
teen edition, though she is only
seven, and we lie on her bed
beneath mosquito netting,
beside the open window, drawing
from the center of the stack.

I ask her: *If you could remove
the bad effects of one food,
what would it be*? And she says,
bread or ice cream, I can't choose,
and I: *same!* and, *it's like*

we're related or something, and she,
laughing, *because we are.*

Then I ask her, *what would you like
to change about the way you look*?
And she says, *I would want to look
more like you*, and I say, *no, I would want
to look more like you.*

And I ask her: *what's the story
behind your first name*?
And she says: *I was named
for a friend of yours*, and
I say, *yes, my oldest friend*,
but don't add, *the one
who almost took you in,
when I didn't think
I could keep you, broke and alone
and at war with your dad.*

It is not the time yet,
I don't think, though I have no
idea when it will be, whether
better to hear it sooner, before
she can fully grasp the implications,
get used to the idea, so it doesn't
come as a surprise, feel
like a betrayal, understands
the most important part:

that I didn't give her up,
couldn't ever.

Newly reading, she asks:
did you ever throw something away
you wish you'd saved?
and I am silent, thanking God,
no, at least nothing irreplace-
able, life-saving, sacred.

And I ask her, *which memories*
of family life will you cherish
when you're older?
And she says: *this one.*

And she asks me: *what is*
the most significant lesson
you've learned in life so far?
And I say: *this one.*

GLEANING

At first I feared
it was want of water,
then lack of light,
that made the leaves
of the basil languish,
but after inquiring
with a friend, I couldn't
but concede it was simply
season's end, time
to harvest what was left,
make pesto of what had been
my greatest success
in the garden yet:

not grown from seed
or even a nursery start,
but a grocery store sleeve
meant to sit on the sill
of the kitchen window,
disposable, almost,
but instead, transplanted
to a galvanized tub in the yard,
it flourished, a bouquet
of fragrance each time
I stepped through the gate,
regenerating after every
trimming until

it didn't, all that remained
now reduced to this
small jar, a jewel
of emerald green,
summer's final
gleaning.

AGAIN TO MEET THE DAY

Early in the morning, late in the season,
I wake to crickets and dark, as if
it were not almost fall, not day at all
but night still, a summer night,
decades ago, when the only ache
I felt was a hunger to become, not this
bone-weariness that makes me
long, more than anything, for another
hour's rest, not to move out into
the world, but to lie here listening
to the sun rise as though, if I tried
hard enough, it could be heard,
as it must be by the birds stirring
even now in their close nests,
forcing themselves again to meet
the day that is given.

VIGIL

On summer nights, decades ago,
I paced the streets
of Honolulu, with you, new-
born, bound to my body
by a long cloth, both of us
swaddled against the vertigo
of a universe expanding
around us—the universe you
were born to, and the one
I was born to when you were
born—breathing in
the perfume of the night-
blooming cereus that grew
out of the volcanic rock-
wall around Punahou, geckos
and mongooses keeping vigil
with us until you finally
fell asleep.

MARSH COVE

Not my childhood home—
I didn't have one of those—
but the house where my children
were children, set back off the road,
on a lot wooded with sweetgums
and juniper, a bank of azaleas
that kept coming back
each time they were cut
down to nubs, and the marsh
behind the house obscenely fecund,
primordial, almost—pluff mud
crawling with crabs, angular shore-
birds perched in snags, the sultry
green of the grass, heat of the days.

The way the palmettos spread
like fans, like hands grasping
at pant legs as you ran
along the boardwalk out
to the island, an Eden for the little
boys you were, lording over this strip
of land, commanders of your fates and then
abandoned to them when
I went for a walk and kept walking.

NEVERTHELESS

In a yard bordered by bamboo
and cypress, a red picket fence,
on a street just off a busier street
that separates her mom's
house from her dad's,
in a town surrounded by mountains
and rivers without end,
in a country divided
by mountains and rivers and fear,
on a planet nearing extinction,
half-burning, half-drowning by turns,
roamed a little girl,

rubbing mint between her fingertips,
deadheading the geraniums,
watering the last of the peppers
and tomatoes though she knew
it was late in the season and soon
they would be through;
sweeping the porch, though
more leaves would fall, the mortar
between the bricks continue to crumble
and crumble to dust.
               Nevertheless,
she somehow felt she must.

What I Left

after Victoria Reidl

I left the laundry and the dishes,
some still in the sink. I left
the endless errands, incessant
needs, not a moment to breathe
or read or think.

I left the late night tirades,
fueled by jug red wine,
fistfuls of my own hair
pulled in desperation.

I left my innocence, theirs.

Our house full of books,
its view of the marsh, that
kitchen where I cooked
a blur of meals, my own
beating heart.

His magnificent mind, their
absolute trust.

What would you leave
if you felt you had to, couldn't
not?

ONCE MORE TO THE LAKE

after Louise Glück

Near every house, there's a path or two.
Near every house, a walk to be taken
around a lake or along a river,
through a city or a park.

In the air, reek of leafmould
and chimney smoke, the season turning.

Like all times, this will both recur and pass:
our strides well-matched, our fingers inter-
laced against the cold, your dog running
ahead, then circling back.

This trail will still exist, north of town,
by the sanctuary, the woods
on one side, a field on the other.
Turtles and cormorants perched
atop long-fallen logs in the water,
goldenrod and asters bright against
late autumn's greens and grays,
empty benches spaced along the way.

Other lovers may rest on them,
other children toddle along
the gravel when this one,
stooping now to grasp a stick,

has grown into a woman
walking alone.

When we stop to kiss,
I hold for a moment
the warm back of your neck,
brush my cheek against
the stubble of your beard,
feel your breath. Peel of geese
wheeling overhead.

SMALL COMFORT

after Katha Pollitt

Tea and books in a warm bed,
rumpled linens, soft from wear,
both cats purring, settling in—too soon
to despair of this life entirely,
entirely too soon to be certain
I will never solve the puzzle
just because I haven't yet.

Attempting for decades and still
not able to make ends meet, still
spending my days in ways I'd rather not, still
wondering what is wrong with me
that it should be this difficult, this tempting
to give up, get out.

But O, these mornings, few
and far between though they may be,
the small comfort they bring:
let the woman in labor, the man
with the chainsaw cutting
his thousandth tree, the child refugee
fleeing she knows not what to
she knows not where, O, let them, too,
lie here in the lamp's glow,
let them know it has not all been,
will not all be, for naught.

AUTUMN REPRIEVE

after Patricia Fargnoli

If you have seen
leaves lit from within
like lanterns in the woods,
littering the ground in mounds
that smell of childhood,
the shuffle-sound
of their silence stirred,
then you have felt hope surge
and known it for its mercy.

And if you have walked
through these woods, up
the steep steps to a rock
ledge where the blue
sky opens, brush strokes
of cloud above the hazy-
layered mountain range,
the valley below a color-
study in hues of hurt and
hunger, then you can attest
to how grace is attained
momentarily, not meant
to be permanent.

The trail continues,
descends,

rises again,
and at the end:
a meadow, golden
and thrumming in the sun,
a log on which to sit
and picnic with friends,
potato chips and sandwiches,
apples and laughter
and for an hour
not a single thought
of the long way
back to your lot.

POMANDER

In hospital
a week before Christmas,
my mother pressed
cloves into oranges
awaiting my birth,
their fragrance filling
the corridors of the surgical-
turned-maternity ward.

And so each year
I do the same: frost
on the window panes,
silence, prick to fingertips
of the thorn-sharp calyx—
a form of penance
for the gift of existing
at all, their perfume a stave
against pestilence and peril
in medieval times, and this

morning I pray
for my own sons, the one
out camping in the cold, the other
broke and broken across town,
that they, too, may sense
a vigil being kept and keep
the faith we all must have

to come into this world
and stay here.

January

Wilted greens and a soft cooked egg.

Chick Corea praying "Someone
to Watch Over Me," then silence.

The ticking of the clock, traffic
a block away, the furnace
quiet momentarily, the house
empty for the first time
in months, stillness
in the very air.

I breathe, exhale, might hear
myself think if I were thinking
but think better of it, picture
instead a field of snow, windswept
in the dusk of a new year.

RETURNING

The studio smells of cold concrete
and clay dust, a kiln firing, the earth
burning. With a wire I slice
a slab of Bella's Blend, cup my hands
and slap it between them, form
a sphere, remove any air
that may be trapped there.

From a deep sink I draw
a bucket of warm water,
choose a sponge, press a pedal
to start the wheel, feel the slip
of a form taking shape, lace
and lock my thumbs, brace
my arms against my sides and press
with all my might, straining
to remember, after decades,
what center felt like,
if I'd even know it if I found it.

FOLLY

We had come to the shore.
You climbed the ramp to the pier
while I took Mara down to the beach
to wade, chase gulls, roll her jeans
higher and higher until it was
no use, and she pounced
like a puppy in the waves.

Eventually, we joined you
and walked the length, past
fishermen casting their lines
into the surf, tourists holding
hands, cowbirds perched or
scavenging for scraps.

When we got to the end, we stared
out at the sea genuflecting in the sun,
and you said, *you would think
we were across from Europe, but
didn't we determine it's actually
Algiers?* And, never a swimmer,
*once, we were here with the boys,
fifteen years ago it must have been,
I walked into the water chest-deep
and thought to myself,* this may be
the last time I do this, *and it was.*

And I said, *maybe*, and you said,
very probably, and I said, *but maybe
not*. We got tacos and,
having beat the crowds, drove
against traffic back toward town,
into the gathering clouds.

COMMENCEMENT

After your performance,
we went for Thai, just
the two of us, at a dive-y
place near my work. You

got fresh rolls, a stir-
fry with basil; I had a cup
of Tom Kha, drunken
noodles with eggplant,
a glass of white wine.

And we spoke of where
you were headed, what
you might study, the apartment
you could get with a friend.

And you looked so handsome
in your new glasses, crisp
white shirt unbuttoned
at the neck, your father's
sadness in your eyes.

Decidedly a man now,
a head above me, whose
hands I'd washed, then watched
move over the trumpet's keys
in disbelief: how can this be

my youngest son, the same one
who only yesterday—but no.

I can't pretend
I didn't see it coming,
didn't know full well that,
if I was lucky, this would be
the beginning.

About the Author

Brit Washburn is the author of the essay collection *Homing In: Attempts on a Life of Poetry and Purpose* (Alexandria Quarterly Press, 2023), and the poetry collection *Notwithstanding* (Wet Cement Press, 2019). She is a graduate of the Creative Writing Program at Interlochen Arts Academy in Northern Michigan, where she was born and raised, and of Goddard College in Vermont. Brit has been awarded an artist's grant by the Vermont Studio Center and for many years served on the boards of the Poetry Society of South Carolina and the Low Country Initiative on the Literary Arts (LILA). She co-directed the salon Poets House South and has worked as a freelance writer, editor, and indexer, a Montessori teacher, and instructor in the Great Smokies Writing Program at University of North Carolina Asheville. The mother of four, Brit is currently a student in the MFA program at Virginia Tech. Her work can be found in print and online via www.britwashburn.com.